Ecosystems of North America

The Prairie

Alison Ormsby

BENCHMARK BOOKS

MARSHALL CAVENDISH
NEW YORK

Series Consultant: Stephen R. Kellert, Ph.D., School of Forestry and Environmental Studies, Yale University

Consultant: Richard Haley, Director, Goodwin Conservation Center

Benchmark Books
Marshall Cavendish Corporation
99 White Plains Road
Tarrytown, New York 10591-9001

Library of Congress Cataloging-in-Publication Data

Ormsby, Alison.
      The prairie / Alison Ormsby.
            p.   cm.—(Ecosystems of North America)
      Includes bibliographical references (p.   ) and index.
      Summary: Examines the prairies of central North America, their ecosystems, and their responses to temperature, weather, and agriculture
      ISBN 0-7614-0897-5 (lib. bdg.)
      1. Prairie ecology—United States—Juvenile literature. 2. Prairie ecology—Canada—
Juvenile literature. [1. Prairie ecology.] I. Title II. Series.
QH104.5.076   1999   97-39444
577.4'4'097—DC21   CIP
                                                                                      AC

Photo Credits
The photographs in this book are used by permission and through the courtesy of:
Animals Animals/Earth Scenes: Richard Day 10; Richard Shiell 14; Charles Palek 30;
Jack Wilburn 36; Bates Littlehales 38; Carol L. Geake 39; Richard Kolar 49; C.C. Lockwood 56.
Grant Heilman Photography: Grant Heilman 4-5, 26-27; Joel Sartore 22; Runk/Schoenberger 50.
Peter Arnold, Inc.: Tom E. Adams 54. *Photo Researchers, Inc.:* Rod Planck front cover, 7;
Dean Krakel II 15; Tom and Pat Leeson 17; Art Rothstein 25; Tom McHugh 31, 59; Larry Miller 32;
Alain Thomas 34-35; David R. Frazier 40; Francois Gohier 42-43; William H. Mullins 45;
James P. Jackson 46; Richard Parker 47; C.K. Lorenz 48. *Tom Stack and Associates:* W. Perry Conway
6; David M. Dennis 18-19; Bill Everett 29; Inga Spence 51-52; John Shaw back cover. Cover design by
Ann Antoshak for BBI.

Series Created and Produced by BOOK BUILDERS INCORPORATED

Printed in Hong Kong
6 5 4 3 2 1

Contents

Seas of Grass

The flowing expanses of tallgrass prairies look like waves of water and are often called seas of grass. Early European pioneers even named their covered wagons prairie schooners after the sailing vessel. As the travelers made their way across the central United States, they felt as if they were crossing an ocean.

Imagine yourself as a visitor to the prairies of Kansas back in the early 1800s. It is easy to lose your way among the big bluestem and Indian grasses, which reach heights of 6 feet (2 m) or more! Beyond the rustling sound of the wind through the grasses, you hear the distant thunder of a herd of bison. Looking up, you catch a glimpse of yellow—a meadowlark's chest as it flashes by. A hawk searching for prey floats high above on outstretched wings. If you look and listen very closely, you may detect the scratching sounds of a badger digging to get a meal. If you turn over the soil with a shovel, you will find signs of the underground activities of insects and burrowing animals like ground squirrels. You will also unearth the extensive roots of grasses strengthening their hold on life.

A sea of Kansas tallgrass stretches into the distance.

With few trees, the western meadowlark builds its nest on the ground, hidden in the thick grass.

Around the world, grasses cover large flat or hilly areas. These grasslands are called pampas in South America, savanna in East Africa, bush in Australia, steppe in Asia, and veld in South Africa. Although all are dominated by grass, each of these grasslands differs in terms of the number of trees, the average temperature, and the amount of moisture. In North America, grasslands are called prairies. Grasslands are generally found in places where there is not enough **precipitation** to support a forest but more than you would find in a desert. Prairies have an average precipitation, in the form of rain, sleet, hail, or snow, of 10 to 39 inches (25–99 cm). If you go to the prairies in the late spring and early summer, you may be drenched by a sudden downpour. Precipitation does not come evenly throughout the year, nor from year to year. Long periods without rain, or **droughts**, often occur. Prairies are known for their warm summers and cold winters in which temperatures can climb as high as 100 degrees Fahrenheit (38° C) in midsummer and drop as low as minus 40 degrees F (-4° C) in winter!

The prairies stretch from the Appalachian Mountains in the East to the Rocky Mountains in the West, and from central Texas to southern Saskatchewan in Canada. Three main types of grassland fill this large region: tallgrass, mixed-grass, and shortgrass. As their names suggest, prairies are distinguished by a difference in the heights of their grasses.

But just as important are the varying levels of available moisture, which help determine the type of grasses that will grow on a

Prairies like this one in Badlands National Park have warm summers and cold winters.

prairie. Two kinds of moisture—precipitation and soil moisture—generally decrease from the eastern to the western United States. In fact, depending on climatic conditions, especially rainfall, the boundaries between prairie types change from year to year. In dry years, for example, the shortgrass prairie may expand to a larger area, then shrink back when precipitation increases. These same conditions—precipitation, soil moisture, and types of grasses and other plants—help determine what animals live in this ecosystem.

What Is an Ecosystem?

Grasslands form an **ecosystem**, plants and animals in a biological community that interact with nonliving parts of the **environment**, such as precipitation and climate. A **community** is made up of all of the organisms that live together and interact in a particular environment, which includes soil, sunlight, and wind. The prairie ecosystem contains many **species**, or kinds, of plants and animals that depend upon each other for survival. Prairie dogs, grasshoppers, burrowing owls, and rattlesnakes are all linked directly or indirecly to the big and little bluestem, blue grama, and buffalo grasses that make up more than half of the plants on the prairie.

Forbs, or broad-leaved plants, are the other widespread type of vegetation. Forbs have deep roots that help them to live in prairies. Often, forbs' roots are even longer than some grass roots. The light-colored, leathery leaves of certain forbs have bristly hairs covering them, which reduce moisture loss from the hot sun. Prairie forbs include colorful flowering plants such as black-eyed Susans and coneflowers. Although there is enough moisture along rivers for some trees to grow, there are very few trees on the dry open prairies. As a result, many birds make their nests on the ground.

Connections

In the prairie ecosystem, the plant and animal species all need a **habitat**, a place to live that has enough of the right kind of food, water, and shelter. Each animal is part of a **food chain**, a feeding relationship in which the path of energy flows from the sun through the species that need this energy to survive.

The Prairie

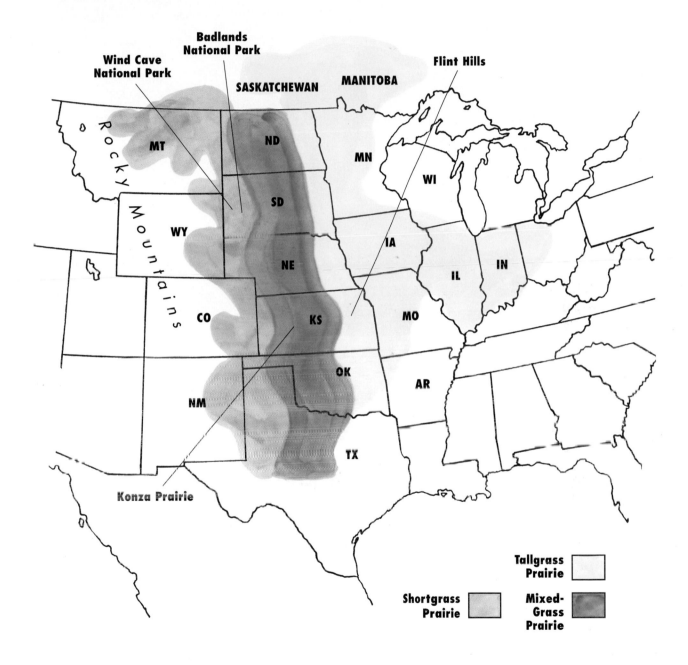

The prairies of North America stretch across the central United States to the Rocky Mountains, and from southern Texas to southern Saskatchewan and Manitoba in Canada.

Coneflowers and black-eyed Susans are forbs that brighten the prairie.

The sun is the original source of energy for all plants and animals. It is, therefore, the starting point for every food chain. Plants
such as prairie grasses use the sun's energy along with water and air
to make their own food through the process of **photosynthesis**. Plants
are **producers**, the only members of the food chain that can make
their own food. The animals in the food chain are called **consumers**,
because they must eat plants or other animals to get their energy.

Animals, such as prairie dogs, bison, and grasshoppers, that
eat only plants are called **herbivores**. The prairie food chain moves
up from herbivores to **omnivores**, which eat both plants and animals, and then to the meat-eating **carnivores**, such as hawks,
spiders, rattlesnakes, and swift foxes. Badgers are omnivores. They
eat fruit, seeds, grass, and small animals such as ground squirrels,
prairie dogs, gophers, and even rattlesnakes! These small carnivores
and omnivores may become **prey** for large meat-eating **predators**,
or hunters, such as coyotes and wolves. The final link in the food

How the Food Web Works

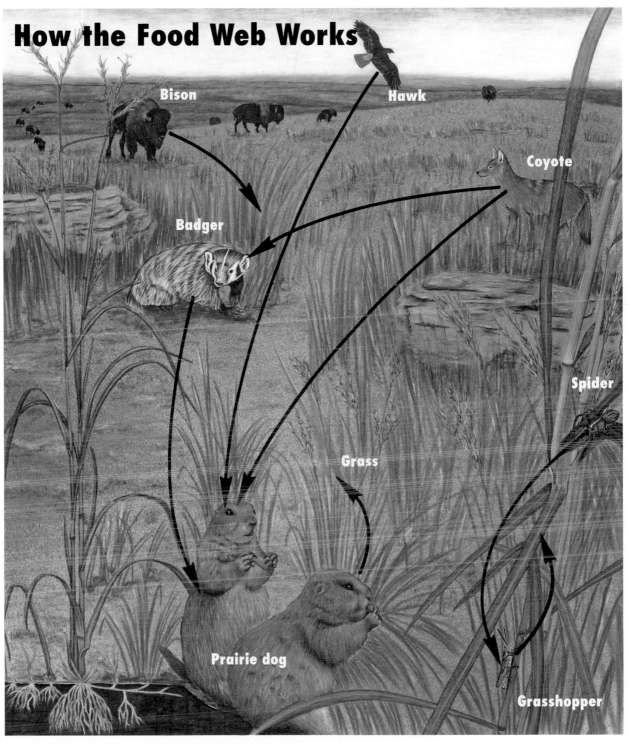

Bison

Hawk

Coyote

Badger

Spider

Grass

Prairie dog

Grasshopper

The interaction among all the food chains in this mixed-grass prairie community is called a food web.

chain is formed by the **decomposers**, such as bacteria and fungi, which eat dead plants and animals.

Animals usually eat more than one kind of food. For example, a burrowing owl may eat young prairie dogs and grasshoppers. So each individual food chain is connected to other food chains to create what is called a **food web**. The food web is an important way in which all of the plants and animals of the prairie are interconnected.

The main element of grasslands is the grass itself, upon which many animals in the prairie food web depend. Grass stems are hollow, which allows them to bend and not break in the prairie winds. Also, some grasses have **rhizomes**, stems that grow just beneath the soil surface. Other grasses have **stolons**, stems that grow above the soil and can sprout away from the original stem when it is burned or eaten. The flowers of grasses are small and not brightly colored like the flowers of forbs.

Many **fossorial**, or burrowing, animals live on the prairie. It helps to live underground, because the open prairies offer few places to hide from predators. Burrowers are also protected from fire and extreme hot or cold weather. Burrows stay warmer than the aboveground temperature in winter and cooler in summer. Burrowing animals also play an important role in helping grass to grow. Their tunnels loosen the soil so that air and water seep into the earth. Perhaps the best-known burrowers of the prairies are the rodents called prairie dogs, whose interconnected burrows form vast underground complexes known as prairie dog towns.

Many physical elements besides plants and animals are connected in the prairie ecosystem. Elements such as water and nitrogen are constantly used and recycled by one community member after another. For example, rain, hail, and snow are absorbed by plants and soil. Prairie animals get moisture from the plants that they eat or by drinking from streams. Some of the water evaporates when it comes in contact with plant surfaces or hot prairie soil. And some water soaks through the soil, where it is then stored underground. The evaporated water returns to the clouds in the big skies of the prairies before again falling to the ground as precipitation. This completes what is called the **water cycle**.

Just as you can trace the path of water in the water cycle, you can follow the path of nitrogen in a food web. Nitrogen in the soil is gathered through grass roots to help plants grow. A grasshopper may eat this grass and in the process take in some of the nitrogen. The nitrogen continues its journey through the food web when a burrowing owl eats the grasshopper. When the owl eventually dies, the nitrogen is returned to the soil by decomposers, such as bacteria and fungi, which break down the owl's body.

What Preserves the Prairies?

Prairies would become forests if it were not for four important factors: precipitation, fire, grazing animals, and wind. Fire often sweeps across the prairies. Long periods without rain lead to drought, which increases the chance of fire. Naturally started by lightning, fire burns the grass aboveground but does not kill the entire plant. Fire returns the nutrients from dried dead plants to the soil. These nutrients help new plants grow.

Over thousands of years, the plants and animals of the prairies have developed **adaptations**, inherited features that enable them to survive changes in their environment. Because grasses grow from their base, they can recover and send up fresh new growth after fire sweeps across the land. However, trees, bushes, and other woody plants grow from the tips of their stems and are killed by the fires.

If you were to walk on the prairie, you might not realize that more of the grass plant is below ground than above. In fact, the roots may be twice as long as the grass you see growing above the ground! Grasses have dense root systems that help them collect moisture and nutrients from the soil. The roots also store energy, which the plant uses to regrow after the part above ground is burned in a fire, frozen during a harsh winter, or eaten by a grazing animal. The complex root systems of prairie grasses also help to hold the soil in place.

Grazers, or grass-eating animals, also help preserve the prairies. These animals, such as bison, snip off the grass near the ground, forcing new grasses to grow. Many of the grazers live together in herds, giving them safety in numbers from predators.

Without fires such as this controlled burn, trees would invade the prairie.

   With few trees to stop it, wind whips across the prairies. These forceful winds help sweep fires to distant prairies. Strong winds are also important carriers of the seeds of grasses, depositing them in new areas where they take root. In forests and other ecosystems, **pollinators** such as birds and insects help plants reproduce by bringing together the pollen from different plants. In the prairie ecosystem, however, wind carries pollen from one plant to another. It also robs plants of their life-giving moisture, so the prairie grasses have developed small leaves that are close together, an adaptation that helps reduce evaporation.

The Changing Prairies

Words often used to describe prairies—*seas of grass*, *endless*, *vast*—bring to mind images of waving grass as far as the eye can see. There once were herds of millions of large, shaggy bison grazing on the North American prairies. Can you imagine what that must have looked like?

In the last 150 years, however, humans have brought dramatic changes to the North American prairies ecosystem. Very little of the original huge expanses of prairie remain. Many of the native grasses have been replaced by cereal crops, such as corn, wheat, oats, and barley. Much of the shortgrass prairie of the western United States has been converted to grazing areas for cattle, which will become food for people. Entire populations of animals, such as bison and prairie dogs, have been almost wiped out.

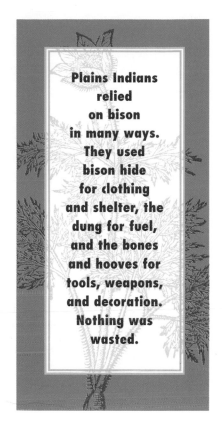

Plains Indians relied on bison in many ways. They used bison hide for clothing and shelter, the dung for fuel, and the bones and hooves for tools, weapons, and decoration. Nothing was wasted.

With few places to hide, this calf is especially vulnerable and huddles close to its mother.

15

Between 1850 and 1910, the bison population fell from 60 million to less than a thousand due to hunting, cattle ranching, and the expansion of railroads. Herds of bison were an easy target as they moved slowly along on the open prairies with nowhere to hide. Railroads brought more hunters to the prairies, as well as settlers, who built towns and farms in the bison habitat. Refrigerated railroad cars also allowed bison meat to be carried to distant markets.

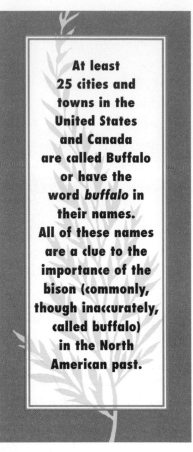

At least 25 cities and towns in the United States and Canada are called Buffalo or have the word *buffalo* in their names. All of these names are a clue to the importance of the bison (commonly, though inaccurately, called buffalo) in the North American past.

For many years, Native Americans had lived in the prairies and used prairie plants and animals in amounts that did not dramatically impact their populations. With new settlers coming to the prairies, everything changed. Bison numbers dropped, upsetting the Native American way of life. The drastic decline in the bison population at the turn of the twentieth century also set off a chain reaction in the food web of the prairie. With the near loss of all bison, a very important grazer was missing from the prairie ecosystem. Grass growth declined because less **organic matter**, decaying plants and animals that help make soil fertile, and nutrients were added to the soil in the form of dung. Less grass meant that other herbivores suffered. Eventually there were fewer prey animals like prairie dogs and jackrabbits for predators such as coyotes.

These were not the only changes in the prairie food web. In the late 1800s, a new large grazer entered the prairie scene: cattle. Cattle replaced bison as the major grazers on the grasslands. Although cattle and bison both eat grass, cattle do not have the same effects on the food web as bison. Cattle graze more selectively and less efficiently than bison, ranging over greater distances and trampling more land to get the same amount of food. In addition, they impact the types of plants that thrive on the prairie. Native grasses are continuously eaten or crushed by the cattle's hooves often cannot grow back. Shrubs that cattle do not like to eat become the only plants that survive. Before bison were hunted

Once believed to be pests, thousands of black-tailed prairie dogs were poisoned by ranchers.

so aggressively, they returned nutrients to the soil through the decomposition of their bodies after death. Most cattle, however, are taken off the land to be used as food. Their removal prevents the return of their nutrients to the food web.

Once cattle were introduced to the prairies, ranchers did all they could to protect their livelihood. Ranchers believed that prairie dogs competed with cattle for food, because they both ate grass. Actually, it would take about three hundred prairie dogs to eat the same amount as one cow! Ranchers tried to wipe out as many prairie dogs as possible by shooting and poisoning them, or by plowing up their burrows. Because prairie dogs prefer to live in overgrazed areas created by cattle ranching, the cattle introduced by humans ended up providing more habitat for these burrowers.

Since large-scale farming and ranching came to the prairies, the efforts of conservation groups have led to some success stories. One example is the comeback of bison. In 1905, William Hornaday of the New York Zoological Society helped form the American Bison Society. This group established two bison reserves: the Wichita Game Preserve and Wind Cave National Park. The society funded captive breeding of remaining bison for release into these protected areas. The original animals are the ancestors of the more than 200,000 bison that roam the prairies today.

Underneath It All

*B*eneath the abundant grasses of the prairies lies unique and incredibly fertile soil. Without this special soil, the prairie would be a desert.

Soil is a mixture of small pieces of rock, microscopic **organisms**, air spaces, drops of water, and organic matter from animal waste products and decaying plants and animals. Over hundreds of years, many prairie grasses and their roots decomposed and accumulated into a thick organic layer near the soil surface. Bacteria, fungi, and tiny insects such as mites break dead plants into small pieces as they eat them. This rich, dark organic matter provides nutrients for new plants to grow. **Topsoil** is the upper, more fertile layer of soil that contains most of the organic matter. Formation of soil is a very slow process; it can take seven thousand years to form an eight-inch (20-cm) layer of topsoil!

Soil Alive!

Among the roots in the soil live many organisms—decomposers and tunneling creatures such as centipedes and worms. Roundworms, or nematodes, in the soil are particularly small. If you carefully placed 50 nematodes end to end, they would measure only

*The activities of earthworms
help create the fertile soil
of the prairies.*

1 inch (3 cm)! The Konza tallgrass prairie in Kansas has up to 500,000 nematodes per square foot (0.1 sq m) in the upper part of the soil.

Decomposers in the soil eat dead plants and animals, releasing the nutrients back into the soil. An earthworm eats this soil that contains decaying plants. It keeps some of the organic part of the soil in its body for its own energy needs. The rest passes through the worm as waste materials, or casts, which also form air spaces that keep the soil loose. Up to 10 percent of the sand, silt, and clay in prairie soils passes through earthworm bodies each year! Earthworms have tiny bristles covering their bodies to help them move through the soil. In addition, the tunnels of earthworms store rainwater, helping to keep soil moist for grasses to use. With up to five million earthworms per acre of soil, that is a lot of tunnels!

Underneath the Grasses

The soil of the prairies is called Mollisol, from the Latin word *mollis*, "soft." The deep, dark, fertile soil layer of the prairies is indeed soft, even when it is dry. Prairie soil in general contains more organic matter than soil in any other ecosystem. Because the soil is so fertile, much of the prairies has been converted to cropland.

Prairie soil is also slightly **alkaline**, or **basic**, meaning its pH is above 7. The **pH** scale is from 0 to 14: 0 is most acidic, 7 is neutral, and 14 is most basic, or alkaline. Orange juice has a pH of 3, and liquid soap has a pH of 11.

The alkaline prairie soils are the perfect environment for bacterial activity and the decay of organic matter. Some forests have acidic soil and have been found to have fewer than one earthworm per square yard (0.8 sq m). In contrast, the Mollisols of prairies can have over five hundred earthworms in an area of the same size. Although prairie soil in general is fertile and alkaline, each of the three prairie types contains slightly different soil.

Special Soils for Unique Conditions

In the tallgrass prairies, the soil is moist year-round. With the thickest layer of organic matter of the three prairie types, this damp soil supports the tall grasses that are characteristic of the region.

Soil Investigation:
How Does Your Soil Compare to Prairie Soil?

The ability for plants to grow depends upon the pH level of their soil. Different plants, including grasses, require different pHs to grow best. Most grasses grow best in basic soil with a pH above seven.

Materials:

- a digging tool
- water
- a container
- litmus paper (or coffee filter paper soaked in cabbage juice)

1. Go outside to your backyard, schoolyard, or a nearby park.

2. Dig up about one tablespoon (15 ml) of soil beneath the grass.

3. Mix the soil with a half cup of water (138 ml)—preferably pure distilled water—and dip half of a strip of litmus paper into it.

What color does the paper turn? If the soil is acidic (pH below seven), the paper will turn pink or red. If your paper turns blue, you have basic (alkaline) soil, which has a pH above seven, like the soil of the prairies.

You can test soil in more than one place and compare your results. After you have tested the soil, be sure to fill in any holes you have made so that the area looks the same as before you began.

Soils in the mixed-grass prairies are not as rich as in the tallgrass region. With less precipitation and shorter grasses, there is less organic matter in the soil. Mixed-grass prairie soil is brown, in contrast to the black tallgrass soil. The mixed-grass prairies also have some low, wet areas and sandy soil. These wet areas are often referred to as prairie potholes. The lakes and wetlands were carved out by glaciers long ago. Now they provide important habitat and rest stops for migrating birds.

Prairie plants have dense roots that hold the soil together and collect moisture.

Soil in the shortgrass prairies is dry and shallow and has very little organic matter, which makes it the lightest in color. The soil may also be rocky or sandy. Near the soil surface is a hard layer of calcium. This hard layer is also present in the mixed-grass prairie, but it is farther below the surface and there is more rich organic soil on top of it. Below the calcium layer, the soil of the shortgrass prairie is always dry. Seeds may sit inactive, or **dormant**, in the shortgrass prairie soil for weeks, months, or years—until there is enough moisture for them to sprout.

Plants of the shortgrass prairies generally have a less extensive root system than those of the other prairie types. But the roots are still larger than the plant aboveground—a grass that is a few inches tall may have four-foot (1-m) roots underground! Shortgrass plants use up all of the soil moisture before the end of the growing season, so grasses dry out in the summer. Because there are no trees and the plants are very short, shortgrass prairies are the windiest prairie type. Being so close to the ground helps shortgrass prairie plants save their moisture and not have as much leaf area exposed to the hot sun and drying winds.

Soil and Settlers

Without the elaborate root system of prairie plants to hold moisture and soil in place, the soil can be carried away by the strong winds that blow across the prairie. This actually happened in the 1930s in the mixed grass prairie region during a long period of drought. Farmers had plowed large areas of land to grow wheat and other grains, breaking up the native grass root system. The combination of drought, intensive farming, and prairie winds caused whole clouds of topsoil to blow away. The fertile soil was gone, and crops could not grow. The region of this tragedy became known as the Dust Bowl. Millions of tons of topsoil blew out of the Dust Bowl states of Kansas, Oklahoma, Texas, New Mexico, and Colorado to places as far away as New York City. In reaction to this event, the Soil Conservation Service was formed by the United States government to prevent similar problems from happening again. The SCS helped farmers use different techniques and educated the public about soil erosion.

People cannot eat the leaves of grasses, but we do eat the seeds. Many of our foods come from grasses that grew wild thousands of years ago and are now used by farmers as food crops. Corn and wheat are two examples. Both crops are grasses grown on the prairies. Corn is grown in areas that were once filled with tallgrass, and wheat is grown in the mixed-grass prairies. Though we do not eat the seeds of wild grasses in the shortgrass prairie, we do eat the cattle that graze there.

Most of the tallgrass prairie has been converted into farmland. Because corn is the main crop grown here, the region is often referred to as the corn belt. In addition to corn, crops such as soybean are grown. Cattle and pigs are also raised, although not as much as in the western shortgrass region. The main agricultural crops are alternated in growing seasons with alfalfa, a legume that helps the soil recover essential nutrients. Corn and other crops, including alfalfa, are often used as **fodder** to feed livestock, including cattle and pigs that will later be eaten by people.

When farmers began to grow more and more crops on the prairies, they realized that after a few years of using the same land, the crops did not grow as well. What they did not know at the time was that the crops were taking necessary nutrients from the soil, and these nutrients were not being replaced. The soil had no time to recover. The grasses that used to live in the soil and contribute to the organic matter and nutrients were gone.

One of the critical nutrients for plant growth is the element nitrogen. Unfortunately, plants cannot just absorb nitrogen from the air. They need the help of special nitrogen-fixing bacteria that take nitrogen from water in the soil. Legumes are plants that have this nitrogen-fixing bacteria in their roots. Legumes such

During the Dust Bowl period, the many dust storms were called black blizzards. Actually, the winds were not blowing dust, but soil. In some places, soil blew into drifts as high as 25 feet (8 m)! Fields could lose 4 inches (10 cm) of topsoil in a two-day storm.

as alfalfa, clover, and soybeans are important because they enrich soil with nitrogen when they decay.

Large-scale, intensive crop production can lead to **soil erosion**, the movement of soil from one place to another. When farmers plow soil to plant seeds, the existing root system is broken up, leaving the loose, bare soil exposed to wind and rain. Erosion occurs when wind and rain carry the loose soil away. Cattle may also cause soil to erode by overgrazing the prairie. This happens when cattle are restricted to one area, eat plants that hold the soil in place, and prevent new plants from growing.

To provide water to help grow crops, managers of large farms use **irrigation** systems. The water used to irrigate crops is often taken from underground reservoirs called **aquifers**, which are limited supplies of water in rocks beneath the soil layers. If too much water on the prairies is used by people and for crops, it may eventually run out.

Huge clouds of soil blackened the sky during the 1930s Dust Bowl.

Fertile Land and Busy Burrowers

he Flint Hills region of eastern Kansas is one of the last places on Earth where you can experience a tallgrass prairie. Flint Hills was named after flint, or chert, a stone that was once used to start fires. Small pieces of chert make up about 75 percent of the soil in some parts of the Flint Hills.

The tallgrass is the moistest prairie, with an average of 30 inches (76 cm) of precipitation each year, mostly in May, June, and July. This prairie community is found in Illinois, western Minnesota, Iowa, Indiana, Missouri, eastern North Dakota, South Dakota, Nebraska, and Kansas, as well as the Canadian provinces of Saskatchewan and Manitoba.

Tall Grasses and Flowering Forbs

The grasses here, dominated by big bluestem and Indian grasses, are the tallest and densest of the prairie grasses. If you stood among them, they would tower over you. Big bluestem grass is also called turkey

A vital part of the prairie ecosystem is found where it cannot be seen—beneath the miles of grass.

claw for the three-branched seed tassel at the top of its flower stalks. In the late summer, you can see these flowers in bloom.

In the wetter areas of the tallgrass prairies, prairie cordgrass grows thick and dense. It gets its nickname "rip gut" from the small spines on the edges of its leaves. In the early spring, the cool-season grasses have a burst of growth—needlegrass with its bristly seeds, Junegrass (which blooms in June), and prairie dropseed, which has tear-shaped seeds.

The grasses in this region are called sod grasses because they have dense roots. These complex roots collect moisture before it flows deep into the soil. The thick root mat and lack of extra moisture near the surface prevents the seeds of trees from getting a hold in the soil. This maintains the prairie ecosystem.

Among the waving big bluestem and Indian grasses, colorful forbs can be found. Delicate white pasque flowers, gold compass plants with its leaves pointing north and south, white-fringed orchids, distinctive yellow or purple coneflowers, black-eyed Susans, and pink blazing stars are among them. Because the tallgrass prairie is the wettest prairie community, some trees can grow here. Especially along rivers where there is plenty of moisture, you may find trees such as cottonwood, American elm, and bur oak reaching toward the sky. The bur oak has leathery leaves and bark that is resistant to fire, so it is well adapted for the tallgrass prairie.

Life Underground

If you were to go to Kansas and visit the tallgrass prairie of the Flint Hills, you might encounter a pocket gopher, ground squirrel, or badger. Notably absent are prairie dogs and pronghorns, two herbivores that are not found in the tallgrass prairie. Actually, your

When settlers moved onto the prairies, there were no trees to cut for lumber to build their homes. Instead, they used available material: sod, the top layer of soil with dense grass roots. The roots of the grass held the blocks of sod together. Sod blocks were stacked to form the walls and ceilings of their homes.

Badgers use their long claws to make burrows and dig after their prey.

chances of getting a good look at a pocket gopher are slim, because
they almost never come above ground except when they are young
or during the mating season. These 7 to 14 inch (18–36 cm) gophers
use their long claws to make burrows that may reach 100 feet (30 m)
in length! Pocket gophers have very small eyes and ears, and each
lives alone in its own burrow. They are so used to life underground
that they cannot stand the sun's heat and will die within one hour
if exposed to it. These gophers eat plant roots underground and
have a very special adaptation: their lips close behind their front

The pasque flower is a forb found in the tallgrass prairie.

teeth so that no soil gets in their mouth while they are digging!

The other burrowing animal specially adapted for underground life in the tallgrass prairies is the ground squirrel. Unlike the pocket gopher, ground squirrels eat grasshoppers and small rodents called voles above ground and use the tall grasses for cover. These grasses also hide the squirrels' burrow entrance. During the cold prairie winters, ground squirrels hibernate to save energy and survive the season. The squirrels' body temperature drops from between 86 and 106 degrees Fahrenheit (30–41° C) to approximately 36 degrees F (2° C)! Also, their heart rate falls from an average of 250 beats per minute to just 5 beats per minute. This drastic slow-down of body functions, called **hibernation**, allows the squirrels to survive on stored fat and avoid the harsh winter conditions aboveground.

Unfortunately for them, pocket gophers and ground squirrels are not entirely safe within their burrows. They have a burrowing predator to contend with, the badger. Badgers, which can grow to almost 3 feet (91 cm) long, have large claws and a flattened

Early settlers made houses out of sod because there were so few trees on the prairie.

body shape to help them dig after prey. If a badger needs to, it is able to dig up to two hours without resting! In addition to burrowing after prey, badgers dig shelters for storing food, resting, and raising young.

These burrowing animals of the prairie—badgers, ground squirrels, and pocket gophers—play an important role in the creation and maintenance of soil. Their burrows create pathways for air and water to penetrate soil, and the burrowing turns over soil to keep it loose. Their waste adds organic matter to enrich the soil.

Grasshoppers are a small part of a very large food web.

The Tallgrass Prairie Today

Of the original 400,000-square-mile (1,036,000-sq-km) expanse of tallgrass prairie in North America, only about 1 percent remains. And these remnants are small, isolated patches. For example, within the Flint Hills region of Kansas lies the Konza Prairie. Like the state name, the Konza Prairie is named after the Kansa Indians who once lived in this area.

The shallow, rocky soils of the Konza Prairie saved the area from farmers, because these soils are not easy to plow. With more than 8,000 protected acres (3,238 ha), this is the largest remaining tallgrass prairie. The Nature Conservancy now owns and manages this property with Kansas State University.

Speed for Survival

If you encounter shorter grasses, fewer trees, and stronger winds than you found in the tallgrass prairie, you are probably in a mixed-grass prairie. The mixed-grass prairie begins at the western edge of the tall-grass prairies. The climate is drier here. During the year, mostly in summer, this region receives only 14 to 24 inches (36–61 cm) of precipitation. With less moisture in the soil, the grasses only grow 2 to 4 feet (61–122 cm) tall. The mixed-grass prairie is often called the Great Plains, and it extends through North Dakota, South Dakota, Nebraska, Oklahoma, central Kansas, and northern Texas.

Bunchgrass and Badlands

In southwestern South Dakota is Badlands National Park, a 380-square-mile (984-sq-km) protected mixed-grass prairie. In addition to the grasses and forbs of the mixed-grass prairie, the Badlands has unique hills and cliff formations, from which the region gets its name. Early visitors thought these were bad lands to cross because of their extreme ledges and valleys. This distinctive appearance is the result of water erosion caused by streams carving into soft

The prehistoric streams that shaped these cliffs have since receded, leaving behind the stark beauty of Badlands National Park.

Bunchgrasses grow in shaggy tufts on the mixed-grass prairie.

soils over millions of years. The rivers flow strongest during the spring snowmelt and summer rainstorms.

Visiting Badlands National Park, you would be sure to see little bluestem grasses. Growing 2 to 3 feet (61–91 cm) tall, this is the main grass type in the mixed-grass prairies. Because winds cause water to evaporate, little bluestem has special methods of holding onto the water it needs. First, wispy tendrils on the undersides of its leaves slow the wind contacting the leaf surface and prevent water from being pulled out of the leaf. Also, the leaves curl up when the weather is dry, so less of the blade is exposed. Little bluestem grows as a bunchgrass, in clumps, unlike the dense sod covering of the grasses on the tallgrass prairie. Bunchgrasses spread to new areas using underground shoots, called rhizomes. Once a rhizome successfully grows out from the parent plant, it sprouts many leaves that grow close together. Other grasses you might find in a mixed-grass prairie like Badlands National Park are Junegrass, needlegrass, and western wheatgrass, another type of bunchgrass.

The Key Is Speed

You might see a swift fox or pronghorn if you have a chance to visit Badlands National Park. These animals are also found in the shortgrass prairies. Both animals have an adaptation especially suited to lands that offer few hiding places—speed.

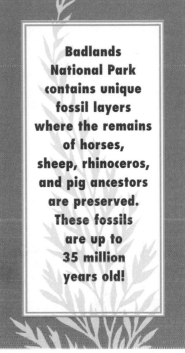

Badlands National Park contains unique fossil layers where the remains of horses, sheep, rhinoceros, and pig ancestors are preserved. These fossils are up to 35 million years old!

The swift fox is a predator. At less than 3 feet (91 cm) long, including its tail, and weighing 4 to 6 pounds (2–3 kg), it is one of the smallest species of fox. Aptly named, the swift fox can reach a speed of 25 miles (40 km) per hour when pursuing prey such as young prairie dogs, jackrabbits, and mice. This solitary animal also has to outrun its own predators within the prairie food chain. The fox may encounter bobcats, coyotes, golden eagles, and wolves. Because swift foxes are **nocturnal**, they are able to use the cover of the night, when they are most active, to hunt and to avoid being eaten! They also have light-colored fur as **camouflage** to blend in with their surroundings. Swift foxes like to use burrows that have already been made by another animal, such as the prairie dog. These foxes use burrows all year, although the males have to move to a new burrow when the female is raising young.

Another animal that you might see in Badlands National Park is the herbivorous jackrabbit. It, too, is a master of speed, able to run as fast as 45 miles (72 km) per hour! The jackrabbit has long, strong hind legs that help it travel to find food and avoid predators. Another adaptation for prairie life is large ears, which help the jackrabbit cool off. Because blood vessels are close to the surface of the ear, having a large ear exposed to the prairie breezes provides the jackrabbit with a natural kind of air conditioning.

The predators of the jackrabbit include coyotes and wolves. Both of these animals suffered when settlers arrived on the prairies.

Millions of coyotes and wolves have been killed because farmers feared that these carnivores would eat their livestock. Once residents of Badlands National Park, wolves are no longer found here. Across the prairies, coyotes have moved into areas where wolves once lived. The jackrabbit population initially rose after their predators were killed in large numbers. But with the recent success of the coyote population, balance has once again been restored in the food web.

The pronghorn is another herbivore of the prairies. It is sometimes called an antelope, but unlike true antelope, such as those of the African grasslands, pronghorns do not have permanent, unbranched horns. The pronghorn gets its name from the male's foot-long (30-cm) horns, which are branched.

Strong legs and large ears are adaptations that make this white-tailed jackrabbit well suited for life on the prairie.

*The pronghorn's speed and
caution were developed millions
of years ago when ancestors
of the cheetah, lion, and hyena
stalked the plains.*

    The pronghorn is the fastest animal in North America. In a
long-distance race, a pronghorn could outrun a cheetah, the fastest
animal in the world. Pronghorns, which can sprint at up to 70 miles
(113 km) per hour, can keep up a speed of 30 miles (48 km) per
hour for many miles. They can outrun any predator because of their
adaptations, including a large windpipe, large heart and lungs, and
strong legs. A pronghorn also holds its mouth open when running
to get plenty of air. In addition to having remarkable speed and
endurance, pronghorns avoid bears, coyotes, bobcats, and other

predators by using their keen eyesight. Very large eyes enable a pronghorn to spot danger up to 4 miles (6 km) away. Once a pronghorn feels the threat of a nearby predator, it shows a rump flash, raising the longer white hairs on its rump to alert the others in its herd. This warning white flash can be seen for miles!

Large areas of mixed-grass prairies are now used to grow wheat. This region of North America is known as the Bread Basket.

People, Prairies, and Pronghorns

When settlers moved to the mixed-grass and shortgrass prairies in the 1800s, there were about 50 million pronghorns. Many were killed for meat. Settlers planted crops in the fertile soil. Wheat became the main crop of the mixed-grass prairies, along with hay to feed livestock. Farmers grazed their cattle in the region and put up more and more fences to mark properties. Although pronghorns are very fast, they are not able to jump over obstacles. Many were killed by running into fences at high speed without seeing them, or by being cut off from water supplies by the fences. In the spring, as the weather turns warmer, herds of pronghorns travel north to fresh feeding areas.

Fences made **migration**, the movement of animals from one place to another, difficult. Many animals perished as a result. By the 1920s, the pronghorn population had dropped to about 13,000. With such reduced numbers, the species faced a permanent end—**extinction**.

Pronghorns are now recovering, partly as a result of conservation efforts, but also because their main predator, the wolf, has been nearly wiped out. The current pronghorn population is approximately 800,000, but the animals have lost much of their former habitat. Conservationists have successfully used live trappings and translocations, directing pronghorns into enclosed areas and then carefully transporting them to prairie locations from which they had once been wiped out. Today, one place in which herds of pronghorns gather in their natural habitat is Badlands National Park.

No Place to Hide

*I*f you do not see any trees, and the plants are very short, you are standing on the driest and windiest prairie type of all—the shortgrass prairie. You can still find these prairies in the western United States.

The shortgrass prairies get less than 12 inches (30 cm) of precipitation per year. That includes an average of four hailstorms! The low rainfall is caused by a **rain shadow** from the Rocky Mountains. Winds in North America generally come from the west, picking up moisture from the Pacific Ocean. As air moves from west to east over the Rocky Mountains, the clouds drop their moisture as rain or snow. Most of the precipitation has fallen before reaching the "shadow" east of the Rockies—the shortgrass prairies of eastern Montana, Wyoming, Colorado, and New Mexico, and northwestern Texas. You are now in the area called the High Plains.

Ready for Dry Times

If you wanted to visit a shortgrass prairie, you could travel to Wind Cave National Park in southwestern South Dakota. Established in 1903, Wind Cave gets its name from one of the world's longest and most complex caves, extending at least 78 miles (126 km)

By slowly grazing their way across the plain, these buffalo are helping the prairie, turning over its rich soil and dispersing seeds stuck in their thick coats.

underground. The park also has 44 square miles (144 sq km) of protected prairie.

Bison, pronghorn, and prairie dogs are plentiful here. And you can see the two most common grasses of the shortgrass prairies: buffalo grass and blue grama. Blue grama is a bunchgrass; up to one hundred stems may come out of a single plant! In contrast, buffalo grass is sod-forming and spreads by stolons, shoots along the ground that may grow 2 to 3 inches (5–8 cm) each day. Buffalo grass reaches heights of 2 feet (61 cm). This grass may have been named because of its ability to grow in the bare ground of abandoned bison wallows. Also, buffalo grass seeds are covered with small spines that catch on the hairs of passing animals. So the bison may have helped spread the seeds of the buffalo grass, which they like to eat!

Other grasses found on the shortgrass prairies are Junegrass, western wheatgrass, needle-and-thread, and red three-awn. Many of the shortgrasses have bristly seeds, which may protect them from seed-eaters and help them to disperse, like the buffalo grass. The spines on the seeds also hold moisture and help the seeds to stay in one place to root.

Shortgrass prairie plants have to respond quickly to changes in available moisture and to cope with periods of drought. These plants include species of cactuses that are often found in deserts and have shallow, widespread roots that are specially designed for dry conditions. These plants are also called **succulents**, because they store water and have juicy tissues. Prickly pear is the most common cactus found on the shortgrass prairies. Many animals, including jackrabbits and coyotes, avoid the spines of the prickly pear and eat its fruits. The seeds of the fruit pass through the animals' digestive systems and are deposited away from the original plant, helping to spread the cactus to new areas.

Yucca is one nongrass plant species found in this area, distinguished by its pointed leaves and long stalk with white flowers. Native Americans used the thick root of yucca plants to make soap. Yucca has a very specialized lifestyle. Pronuba moths feed on the seeds of yucca, live only in yucca flowers, and are its only known pollinators.

Needle-and-thread grass blows in the winds of the shortgrass prairie.

The shortgrass prairie is home to only a few woody plants, or shrubs. Sagebrush, with its characteristic silvery-gray leaves, is a shrub that grows well in overgrazed areas. Woody plants are the preferred food of herbivorous pronghorn and mule deer. Both species are **browsers**, which mainly eat woody plants. Grazers, however, eat grass, so the pronghorn and mule deer do not directly compete for food with the bison, which prefer grass. As they walk and eat, bison turn up the soil, helping to create places for new seeds to grow and fertilizing the soil with their waste. (Bison are often called buffalo, or American buffalo, but American bison are not related to the African Cape buffalo or the Asian water buffalo.)

Shortgrass prairies have very few forbs. The forbs here have longer roots than the grasses. Many taste bad or may even be poisonous to cattle, so forbs are more common in overgrazed areas. Forbs

In addition to soap, Indians made sandals, mats, and baskets out of yucca fibers and ate the fruit and flowers.

of Wind Cave National Park and other shortgrass prairies include red false mallow, purple loco, western wallflower, and curlycup gumweed, named for its sticky flower head. The shrubs and forbs of the shortgrass prairies have light-colored leaves with protective coatings, such as a fuzzy surface to reduce evaporation and reflect the sun's rays.

Gumweed, a forb of the shortgrass prairie, is named for its sticky flower heads.

Master Burrowers

Animals of the shortgrass prairies have few places to hide aboveground. Prairie dogs, which also live in mixed-grass prairies, thrive in shortgrass prairies like Wind Cave National Park. Prairie dogs are actually a kind of ground squirrel; they got the name *dog* from the barking sound that they make to communicate. Herbivorous prairie dogs do not have to worry that there is very little water available. They rarely drink, because they get enough water from their food.

Prairie dogs are **colonial**—they live in groups in large burrow complexes. These colonies, or towns, may reach 10 feet (3 m) deep and are made of many interconnected chambers. The dirt that these exceptional burrowers have dug to build their tunnels is shaped into a mound around the outside of the entrances; the mound prevents rainwater from flooding the tunnels. Prairie dogs are less numerous than they once were, and their towns today do not spread as far as those in the past. One remarkable prairie dog colony of the early

Burrowing owls often live in dens that prairie dogs have dug.

1900s covered approximately 24,000 square miles (62 sq km). It was thought to be home to 400 million prairie dogs!

Prairie dogs are not the only dwellers in their active towns. Many other animals depend upon prairie dog burrows for a place to live or for hunting grounds. Some animals that share the towns are ground-nesting birds such as the horned lark, killdeer, and mountain plover. Burrowing owls live in prairie dog burrows. These small birds do not often hunt prairie dogs, although they may eat a young prairie dog. In turn, prairie dogs may eat owl eggs. Such shifting relationships are all part of the prairie food web.

Prairie dogs often stand watch by their burrow entrances. They keep the grass close-cropped for a clear view of the prairie and the many predators that come from all directions—hawks and eagles overhead, rattlesnakes and foxes from the ground. Omnivorous badgers, which eat both plants and animals to survive, prey on prairie dogs and can dig out a prairie dog

The black-footed ferret is the most endangered mammal in North America. Black-footed ferrets have a very specialized diet—their main food is prairie dogs! When the prairie dogs' numbers dropped as a result of human activities, black-footed ferrets lost their food supply and almost became extinct. There are now captive breeding programs to help the ferret population, and some have been reintroduced to their natural habitat in Badlands National Park.

burrow in minutes. When a prairie dog spots danger, it gives a repeated, high-pitched warning call. The call is passed along, and in no time, the prairie dogs have vanished underground. Of course, all the other prey animals know what the prairie dogs' call means, and they seek safety, too.

Bison and prairie dogs do not have a predator-prey relationship, though they do depend on each other indirectly. Bison are among the herbivores that graze on the grasses in and around the prairie dog towns. By keeping the grasses low, bison help prairie dogs watch out for predators more easily. As bison graze, the herds

While offering great protection, living underground is not the perfect solution. The black tailed prairie dogs have to come out sometime.

Harvester ants form large colonies on the shortgrass prairie. These worker ants are creating separate chambers to shelter eggs, larvae, and pupae.

create wallows. In their wallows, bison bathe in the dirt, coating their fur with dust. It is believed that the dust helps keep mites and other insect pests from bothering the bison. Prairie dogs often use these already-cleared wallows to create new burrows.

Harvester ants are another species that may share prairie dog towns, making their own colonies 6 to 10 feet (2–3 m) underground. These colonies of harvester ants can contain up to ten thousand ants. The ants build the doorways of their colonies facing southeast to avoid the strong summer winds coming from the northwest. They are called harvester ants because they collect seeds from the grasses and store them in underground chambers.

Grazing the Shortgrass

It might seem that shortgrass prairies are too dry for farming. But one cereal grass, millet, can be planted because it can survive periods of drought. The harvested millet grain is often fed to cattle, which graze on the shortgrass prairies. The cattle herds are often very large and confined to one area. Because the grass may not have time to grow back each year, cattle might overgraze a given area, which in turn leads to soil erosion. Unlike the situation in the other prairie types, grazing has a greater impact here than fire. If action is not taken to allow the grasses to grow back, such as by moving cattle to a new area, the shortgrass prairie may suffer permanent damage.

Tomorrow's Prairie

*W*e depend on prairies for many of our foods, such as corn, wheat, barley, rice, oats, and rye. Farming has changed from a family operation to agribusiness, a large-scale business using hundreds of acres of land. Instead of the great variety of grasses that used to live on the prairies, these large farms often grow one plentiful crop, a practice known as **monoculture**. These single crops are vulnerable to disease and drought and cannot recover as fast as the diverse native prairie grasses.

Modern machinery for huge agribusinesses causes soil compaction, which results in the loss of important air spaces in soil. Without these spaces, water cannot flow easily into the soil. The yearly plowing of fields may also lead to soil erosion.

Pressure on the Prairie

Pesticides kill insects or small mammals, and **herbicides** target unwanted plants, often referred to as weeds. These killing agents are widely used by agribusiness, but they affect more than the targeted animals and plants. In addition to killing undesirable insects, pesticides often kill beneficial insects that

This massive combine quickly and efficiently harvests a field, but it also poses a potential long-term threat to the prairie.

happen to be in the treated area. The poisons also build up as they travel up the food chain. A bird that eats many insects will accumulate the poisons in its body. A predator that eats many poisoned birds will have even more of the poison in its body. One way to reduce dependency on harmful chemicals is **integrated pest management (IPM)**, which uses insect species to control crop pests. This technique uses specific predator insects to eat undesired insects. For example, some nematodes are **parasites**, they eventually kill their insect host. Controlled releases of nematodes kill the

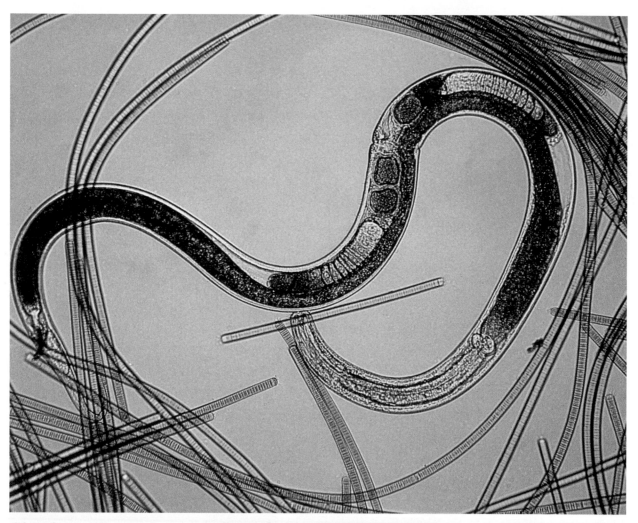

Often, the use of nematodes is more effective than spraying harmful pesticides.

Soil and Sod *vs.* Water and Wind

Wind and rain are two climatic features that affect the prairies, especially when the native grasses are plowed to grow crops or are eaten by livestock. The grasses of the prairie are specially adapted to the conditions of their environment. Without them, the prairie soil is vulnerable to erosion. To see the impact of wind and rain on different surface areas, try the following experiment.

Materials:

- a small pan of soil
- a piece of sod (0.1 sq m)
- a few cups of water
- an electric fan

What do you expect will happen if you pour water on two different areas, one of bare soil and the other a grassy area? What do you think would happen to the same areas if you blew a fan on them?

1. Start by carefully placing your pan of soil in front of a gently blowing fan. Before you begin, make sure the area is clean and you have laid down some paper to catch the soil if it blows away.

2. Observe what happens when the blowing air hits the soil. (You will not need to have the fan on a high setting to get results.) Once you have tried the effects of wind on the bare soil, turn the fan onto the piece of sod (grass and soil). Record your observations.

3. Next take the pan of soil and pour one cup (275 ml) of water on it. What happens? Take the pan and tilt it slightly. Pour another cup of water onto it. Does the soil move? Try the same thing with the piece of sod. Do you notice any difference?

In the past forty years, the aquifer beneath Kansas has dropped over 50 feet (15 m) due to irrigation.

target insect, not the other harmless insects or plants that happen to be in the treated area.

As more and more people move to prairie areas and as more food crops are grown there, the demand for water continues to rise. Irrigation is needed to water crops and for human use, such as drinking water. The Ogallala aquifer, North America's largest underground reservoir of water, is named after the Sioux tribe that once inhabited part of the area it covers. The aquifer stretches from beneath Texas to Nebraska and is rapidly being used up—billions of gallons of water are pumped out of it each year. About 90 percent of the water taken from the Ogallala aquifer is used for irrigation! In 1950, the aquifer under Kansas was 58 feet (18 m) deep. By 1990 the level had dropped drastically to 6 feet (2 m) deep. At current rates of water use, this important aquifer may be pumped dry in the next twenty years.

Hope for the Future

New methods of agriculture promise to lessen the destructive impacts farming has previously had on the soil and on native plants and animals. Crop rotation, growing different crops or mixed crops on plots of land over the years, can help the soil recover its nutrients. If a cereal grain such as corn or wheat is alternated with a legume such as alfalfa or clover, essential nitrogen will be returned to the soil. It is also helpful to leave a field unplanted, or **fallow**, for a growing season. Another prairie-saving strategy is contour plowing, planting and harvesting with the natural curves of the gently rolling prairie hills. This prevents rain from washing soil down hillsides.

In areas where cattle are raised, one way to minimize their impact is through controlled or rotational grazing. Overgrazing is avoided by moving cattle from place to place to keep them out of sensitive areas and give the grazed plants time to recover and grow back.

Prescribed burns are being conducted by conservation organizations, such as The Nature Conservancy, to regenerate native prairie ecosystems. In the past century, most prairie fires have been suppressed, so the dead grasses are abundant and trees are starting to invade prairie habitat. Bringing back carefully planned fires prevents the further advance of trees into the prairie ecosystem and rejuvenates the native grasses.

In addition to controlled burning, many conservation organizations are making efforts to restore the prairie. Seeds of native prairie species are collected from healthy grasslands and are planted in original prairie land that had been used as farmland or otherwise depleted. In some of the restored areas, the establishment of original grasses has already led to the return of native animal species, such as Eastern bluebirds, meadowlarks, bobolinks, falcons, coyotes, and foxes. This sparks the hope that someday the prairies will once again cover large areas of North America, and we will all have a chance to walk among the swaying grasses and hear the howl of a wolf or the call of a horned lark.

Plains Indians set prairie fires on purpose to help the grasses grow, because they depended on the bison that needed the grasses for food. One Native American name for fire reveals the connection between fire and bison: "red buffalo."

Pronghorn and bison graze together again on the prairie.

Glossary

adaptation an adjustment or special feature that helps an organism survive *in its habitat, or environment.*

alkaline having a pH above 7; basic.

aquifer an underground reserve of water with rocks, sand, and gravel.

basic having a pH above 7; alkaline.

browser an animal that eats mostly shrubs, a type of woody plant.

camouflage blending in with the surroundings through color or behavioral modification.

carnivore an animal that eats only other animals.

colonial living in a group of the same species.

community all of the organisms that live together and interact in a particular environment.

consumer an animal that eats other animals or plants.

decomposer an organism that gets its energy by breaking down dead plants and animals. Bacteria and fungi are decomposers.

dormant inactive and seemingly lifeless but capable of becoming active.

drought an extended time of little or no precipitation.

ecosystem an interacting and interdependent community of plants, animals, and their physical environment.

environment all the living and nonliving things that surround an organism and affect its life.

extinction the state in which no member of a species remains.

fallow not in use, as in an unplanted field.

fodder food for livestock animals, such as cattle, sheep, and horses.

food chain a term used to describe feeding relationships in which one organism is eaten by another organism, which in turn is eaten by a larger organism.

food web many interconnected food chains representing the feeding links among community members.

forb a non-woody leafy plant, not including grasses.

fossorial adapted for digging and living underground in a burrow.

grazer an animal that eats mostly grass.

habitat an area containing the food, water, and shelter needed for an animal to live; an animal's home.

herbicide a chemical used to kill plants.

herbivore an animal that eats only plants.

hibernation a dormant state during which an animal's metabolism slows to aid in surviving harsh seasons.

integrated pest management (IPM) methods of controlling unwanted insects and plants without harming other organisms, such as through the use of natural predators.

irrigation the artificial application of water to land to assist in the production of crops.

migration movement of animals from one region to another.

monoculture a single large crop.

nocturnal active during the night.

omnivore an animal that eats both plants and other animals.

organic matter decaying dead plants and animals that help make soil fertile and give it a dark color.

organism any living thing.

parasite a plant or animal that lives on or in another, feeds on its host, and is harmful to it.

pesticide a chemical used to kill insects or animals.

pH measure of acidity or alkalinity on a scale of 0 to 14 with 7 being neutral; acids have a pH below 7 and bases have a pH above 7.

photosynthesis the process by which plants make their own food by using sunlight, carbon dioxide, and water.

pollinator something, such as wind, insects, birds, and bats, that brings pollen to plants, enabling them to reproduce.

precipitation water that falls as rain, sleet, hail, or snow.

predator an animal that kills and eats other animals (prey).

prey an animal that is eaten by other animals (predators).

producer an organism, such as a plant, that makes its own food from the sun's energy.

rain shadow an area downwind from mountains that receive very little precipitation.

rhizome a horizontal underground stem.

soil erosion the movement of soil by wind or water.

species a group of organisms that closely resemble each other and can breed with each other to produce fertile offspring.

stolon a horizontal stem above ground.

succulent type of plant adapted to live in dry areas by having small or no leaves and storing water.

topsoil the uppermost, fertile soil layer.

water cycle process by which water is transformed from vapor in the atmosphere to precipitation on land and water surfaces and ultimately back into the atmosphere.

Further Exploration

Books

Brown, Lauren. *Grasslands*. New York: Alfred A. Knopf, 1997.

Cushman, Ruth Carol, and Stephen R. Jones. *The Shortgrass Prairie*. Boulder, CO: Pruett Publishing Company, 1988.

Encyclopaedia Britannica. *Prairie Animals*. Chicago: Encyclopaedia Britannica, Inc., 1979.

Flint, David. *The Prairies and Their People*. New York: Thomson Learning, 1993.

Lambert, David. *Our World: Grasslands*. Englewood Cliffs, NJ: Silver Burdett Press, 1987.

Sayre, April Pulley. *Grassland*. New York: Twenty-First Century Books, 1994.

Staub, Frank. *America's Prairies*. Minneapolis, MN: Carolrhoda Books, Inc., 1994.

Organizations

Badlands National Park
P.O. Box 6
Interior, SD 57750
(605) 433-5361

Konza Prairie
Division of Biology, Ackert Hall
Kansas State University
Manhattan, KS 66506
(913) 587-0441

The Land Institute
2440 E. Water Well Road
Salina, KS 67401
(913) 823-5376

The Nature Conservancy
1815 North Lynn Street
Arlington, VA 22209
(703) 841-5300 or (800) 628-6860

The Nature Conservancy
Tallgrass Prairie Preserve
P.O. Box 458
Pawhuska, OK 74056
(918) 585-1117

United States Department of Agriculture
Soil Conservation Service
Room 0054 South
Washington, DC 20250
(202) 720-5157

Wind Cave National Park
Route 1, Box 190
Hot Springs, SD 57747
(605) 745-4600

Index

Page numbers for illustrations are in **boldface**.